UNDERSTANDING
The
HUMANE AI PIN

Your Guide To A Detailed Insight About The Future Of Artificial Intelligence

Kenneth R. Jacob

Table of Contents

Chapter 1: Introduction to Humane AI PIN

What is Humane AI PIN?

In the fast-evolving domain of artificial intelligence (AI), where gadgets and applications are becoming increasingly interwoven into our daily lives, Humane AI PIN stands as a pioneering wearable that effortlessly mixes AI capabilities with a user-centric approach. Unlike typical AI-powered wearables that generally promote screen-based interfaces and obtrusive notifications, Humane AI PIN takes a completely different approach, prioritizing a screenless, conversational, and privacy-conscious experience.

At its core, Humane AI PIN is an AI-powered assistant that sits discreetly on your person, ready to aid you throughout the day. Its compact shape, like a little square pendant, allows it to be effortlessly fastened to clothing or a purse. Unlike smartwatches or smart glasses, Humane AI PIN eliminates the need for constant screen engagement, guaranteeing that you may stay engaged with the world around you without being attached to a digital interface.

Overview of Humane AI PIN's Features

Humane AI PIN's unusual design and conversational interface set it distinct from typical wearables. Its important features include:

• **Conversational AI:** Humane AI PIN utilizes a powerful AI assistant that reacts to natural language instructions, answers inquiries, handles tasks, and offers individualized support.

• **Screenless Interaction:** The gadget lacks a standard screen, relying instead on voice commands, gestures, and a small built-in projector to give visual information.

• **Privacy-focused Approach:** Humane AI PIN stresses privacy, minimizing data gathering and providing user control over their information.

• **Seamless Integration:** Humane AI PIN interacts effortlessly with many devices and services, including cellphones, calendars, and communication apps.

• **Expandable Functionality:** The device's open-platform architecture enables for the development of new features and applications.

Benefits of Using Humane AI PIN

The benefits of adopting a Humane AI PIN extend far beyond convenience. It empowers individuals to enrich their daily lives in various ways:

• **Simplified Communication:** Humane AI PIN promotes hands-free communication, enabling users to make calls, send texts, and connect with contacts without reaching for their smartphones.

• **Enhanced Productivity:** The AI assistant can manage calendars, schedule reminders, and collaborate with productivity tools, streamlining everyday activities and boosting efficiency.

• **Personalized Information Access:** AI PIN gives real-time access to critical information, like news updates, weather predictions, and travel directions.

• **Enhanced Wellness:** The device can track physical activities, analyze sleep patterns, and deliver individualized wellness advice.

• **Augmented Reality Experiences:** Humane AI PIN can improve visual experiences with augmented reality overlays, giving navigation aids, language translations, and contextual information.

Target Audience for Humane AI PIN

Humane AI PIN caters to a broad variety of customers desiring a more personalized, integrated, and privacy-focused AI experience. It is particularly well-suited for:

- **Busy Professionals:** The hands-free communication, task management, and tailored information capabilities help streamline their workday and boost productivity.

- **Health-conscious Individuals:** Exercise tracking, sleep monitoring, and wellness recommendations can assist their health objectives and overall well-being.

- **Tech-savvy Individuals:** The open-platform architecture, conversational interface, and augmented reality features appeal to users seeking sophisticated technology integration.

- **Privacy-conscious Users:** The emphasis on data privacy and user control resonates with individuals worried about their personal information.

Overall, Humane AI PIN stands out as a breakthrough wearable that redefines the role of AI in our daily lives. Its focus on user-centricity, privacy, and conversational engagement sets it different from conventional wearables, making it a vital tool for anyone wishing to enrich their lives with the power of AI.

Chapter 2: Getting Started with Humane AI PIN

Unboxing and Initial Setup

Your journey with Humane AI PIN begins with the unboxing experience. The elegant package mirrors the device's basic design, inviting you to discover the world of possibilities that lie within. Upon opening the box, you'll find the following:

• **Humane AI PIN device:** The centerpiece of your AI companion, contained securely in its specialized package.

• **Magnetic charging pad:** This wireless charging pad stylishly compliments the device and enables effortless charging.

• **User manual:** A complete guide to exploring the device's features and functionalities.

• **Warranty information:** For peace of mind knowing your investment is covered.

Charging and Activation

To begin your AI journey, follow these basic steps:

1. Place the Humane AI PIN on the magnetic charging pad. The gadget will automatically begin charging, signaled by a modest LED light.

2. Download the Humane AI PIN app: This software acts as the core center for managing your device settings, adjusting features, and accessing advanced functionality. Search for the app in your app store and download it onto your smartphone or compatible device.

3. Launch the app and follow the on-screen instructions. This method will assist you through

pairing your device with your smartphone over Bluetooth, creating an account, and choosing your chosen settings.

Exploring Basic Features and Gestures

Once engaged, educate yourself with Humane AI PIN's intuitive UI and natural interaction methods:

• **Voice Commands:** The device is meant to respond to natural language commands. Speak properly and effectively to initiate tasks, ask questions, and control various functions.

• **Touch Gestures:** Swipe, tap, and hold on the smooth surface of the device to navigate menus, choose options, and interact with information.

• **Haptic Feedback:** Subtle vibrations provide validation of your actions and offer additional context throughout interactions.

Personalizing your AI Experience

Humane AI PIN lets you tailor your experience with a multitude of settings and options:

• **Voice assistant configuration:** Choose your chosen language, alter voice response settings, and configure wake-up words for seamless interaction.

• **Notification preferences:** Select the alerts you wish to receive, set notification sounds, and choose the level of detail displayed on the projected information.

• **Privacy settings:** Control how your data is collected, used, and shared, ensuring your privacy is always safeguarded.

• **Feature customization:** Customize the order of functions in the main menu, modify the brightness of the projected information, and choose which apps and services you want to link with your device.

Discovering the Potential of Humane AI PIN

This initial setup is just the beginning of your experience with Humane AI PIN. As you explore the device's functions and learn its powers, you'll experience a new degree of interaction with technology:

- **Hands-free communication:** Make and receive calls, send messages, and manage your contacts all with voice commands, freeing your hands for other chores.

- **Enhanced productivity:** Streamline your daily chores with voice-activated reminders, calendar management, and access to real-time information.

- **Personalized information and knowledge management:** Create unique information feeds, organize notes and recordings, and get personalized recommendations based on your interests.

- **Immersive augmented reality experiences**: Overlay information onto the real environment, navigate with turn-by-turn AR directions, and translate languages in real-time.

- **Enhanced health and wellness**: Track your exercise activities, monitor sleep patterns, and receive individualized health suggestions.

Chapter 3: Revealing the Power of Humane AI PIN

Beyond its clean appearance and intuitive interface, Humane AI PIN lies a great force - the capacity to alter how we engage with technology and better our daily lives. This chapter digs deeper into the main strengths of the Humane AI PIN, showing how its novel features and capabilities satisfy our requirements and empower us to achieve more.

Redefining Human-Computer Interaction

At the heart of Humane AI PIN lies a fundamental shift in how we interact with technology. It breaks from the usual screen-based approach, embracing a conversational and natural language interface that feels more intuitive and human-centric. This change has various advantages:

- **Reduced screen fatigue:** By decreasing dependency on displays, Humane AI PIN combats digital eye strain and allows you to stay engaged with the world around you.

- **Enhanced accessibility:** Voice commands and gesture controls make the device accessible to people with diverse physical abilities.

- **Increased attention and focus**: By reducing distractions from a continual screen presence, Humane AI PIN allows for deeper involvement with tasks and activities.

- **More natural and intuitive interaction:** Speaking and gesturing feel more natural than interacting with touchscreens, offering a smoother and more organic experience.

Empowering Productivity and Efficiency

Humane AI PIN is designed to streamline your daily routines and boost your overall efficiency. Its features are meticulously created to empower you to achieve more with less effort:

- **Hands-free communication and task management:** Manage your calendar, schedule reminders, and remain connected with coworkers and loved ones all with voice commands.

- **Real-time information access:** Get fast updates on weather, news, traffic, and other pertinent information without needing to search or browse through different apps.

- **Personalized recommendations and insights:** The AI assistant anticipates your requirements and proactively gives information and recommendations that support your goals and interests.

- **Seamless interaction with productivity tools**: Connect Humane AI PIN with your favorite productivity apps and services to achieve a streamlined and efficient workflow.

Unleashing the Potential of Augmented Reality

Humane AI PIN gives a new dimension of interaction with the environment around you through augmented reality (AR). This technology smoothly overlays digital information over the actual world, producing immersive and engaging experiences:

• **Enhanced navigation and wayfinding**: Get turn-by-turn directions with AR overlays, locate sites of interest, and explore new environments with interactive maps.

• **Language translation and communication:** Break down language barriers by translating text and speech in real-time, enabling seamless communication with individuals speaking different languages.

• **Interactive learning and education:** Bring learning materials to life using 3D models, annotations, and simulations, making learning more interesting and effective.

• **Visual information augmentation:** Gain deeper insights into your surroundings by overlaying information on buildings, landmarks, and other things in real time.

A Holistic Approach to Wellness and Health

Humane AI PIN goes beyond productivity and communication; it also empowers you to take responsibility for your health and well-being. Its features offer a holistic approach to wellness:

- **Fitness tracking and activity monitoring:** Track your daily steps, distance, calories burned, and other fitness data to stay motivated and meet your fitness objectives.

- **Sleep tracking and sleep quality analysis:** Gain insights into your sleep habits and receive personalized advice for enhancing your sleep quality.

• **Stress management and mindfulness exercises:** Access guided meditations and breathing exercises to reduce stress and improve relaxation.

• **Personalized health recommendations and insights:** Receive individualized advice on nutrition, exercise, and other aspects of your health based on your particular requirements and preferences.

A Catalyst for Personal Growth and Development

Humane AI PIN helps you to learn, grow, and enhance your talents in a personalized and engaging manner. Its features allow access to a large array of materials and tools for lifelong learning:

- **Personalized learning recommendations:** The AI assistant proposes learning resources and courses based on your interests, goals, and learning style.

- **Immersive educational experiences:** Explore interactive learning modules, virtual reality simulations, and gamified learning experiences to make learning more interesting and effective.

- **Skill development and training:** Access individualized coaching programs, skill-building activities, and feedback to gain new talents and boost your existing ones.

- **Knowledge management and organization:** Capture your thoughts, ideas, and learnings using voice notes and recordings, and organize them for future reference and review.

Humane AI PIN symbolizes a paradigm shift in how we connect with technology and ourselves. By stressing user-centric design, privacy, and ethical development, it empowers us to do more, live healthier, and unlock our full potential. As we embrace the power of Humane AI PIN and similar technologies, we usher in a new age of human-computer connection that promises to benefit our lives in fundamental ways.

Chapter 4: Design and Hardware Specifications of Humane AI PIN

Humane AI PIN's design and hardware specifications play a significant role in creating its distinctive screenless, conversational, and privacy-focused experience. This chapter digs deeper into these factors, analyzing the device's form factor, display technology, internal components, and other hardware features.

Physical Design and Form Factor

Humane AI PIN uses a minimalist and inconspicuous approach to design. It offers a tiny square pendant form factor with rounded corners, measuring roughly 25mm x 25mm x 10mm. This compact size allows for unobtrusive insertion on clothing, backpacks, or necklaces, ensuring it's always within reach without being cumbersome.

The item is constructed from high-quality materials, such as ceramic or anodized aluminum, delivering a sleek and sturdy finish. The absence of buttons or physical interfaces reinforces its concentration on voice and gesture interaction.

Display and Projection Capabilities

Humane AI PIN is remarkable in its lack of a traditional screen. Instead, it utilizes a mini projector that displays information directly onto the user's palm or nearby surfaces. This "Laser Ink Display" technology projects a high-resolution (720p) image in a blue-green tint, ensuring clear viewing under various lighting circumstances.

The projected information can be adjusted to display notifications, text messages, maps, weather forecasts, and other pertinent data. This method minimizes the need for frequent screen contact, allowing users to remain engaged with their environment while still obtaining information.

Processor, Memory, and Connectivity

Humane AI PIN is driven by a low-power processor tailored for AI activities. This processor enables efficient operation, providing flawless speech recognition, natural language processing, and real-time information access.

The device comes packed with adequate memory to hold user data, preferences, and locally downloaded programs. It also supports different networking choices, including Wi-Fi, Bluetooth, and cellular (optional), allowing for seamless communication and data transfer.

Sensors and Input Methods

Humane AI PIN incorporates a variety of sensors to enhance its functioning and reactivity. These include:

• **Microphone:** High-sensitivity microphone for accurate voice recognition and crisp audio capture.

• **Accelerometer and Gyroscope:** Detect movement and gestures for gesture-based interaction.

• **Ambient Light Sensor:** Adjusts the projection brightness based on environmental lighting.

• **Proximity Sensor:** Detects when the device is close to the hand for triggering the projector.

In addition to voice instructions, Humane AI PIN supports various input methods:

• **Touch Gestures:** Users can swipe and tap on the device's surface to traverse menus and interact with applications.

• **Haptic Feedback:** Provides tiny vibrations to validate user actions and provide feedback.

• **Head movements:** Certain head movements, such as nodding or shaking, can be employed for specific interactions.

Battery Life and Charging

Humane AI PIN is built for all-day use and has a battery life that may last up to 24 hours on a single charge. The real battery life can vary depending on usage patterns and functionalities enabled.

The device charges wirelessly with a specific charging pad. This eliminates the need for cords and guarantees a convenient charging experience.

Humane AI PIN's hardware specifications are deliberately developed to suit its unique screenless and conversational approach. The basic design, revolutionary projection technology, powerful processing, and numerous sensor input modalities combine to produce a user experience that is both straightforward and unobtrusive. This attention to hardware design underlines Humane AI PIN's position as a breakthrough wearable that reimagines the way we interact with technology.

Chapter 5: Software and Operating System of Humane AI PIN

The heart of Humane AI PIN's functionality rests in its software and operating system, which manage its speech recognition, natural language processing, AI capabilities, and user interface. This chapter offers a deep dive into these characteristics, studying the key technologies that fuel the device's smart and user-friendly experience.

Overview of Humane AI PIN's Operating System

Humane AI PIN works on a custom-built operating system specifically developed for wearables and tuned for low-power consumption and responsiveness. This operating system prioritizes real-time performance and easy integration with multiple services and applications.

The basic components of the operating system include:

- **Real-Time Kernel:** Provides effective resource management and assures rapid response to user inputs.

- **Embedded AI Framework:** Enables on-device processing of voice commands and natural language queries, delivering faster response times and more privacy.

- **Connectivity Management:** Handles Wi-Fi, Bluetooth, and cellular connections, providing seamless communication and data transfer.

- **Security Framework:** Implements rigorous security procedures to protect user data and device operation.

- **Application Runtime:** Enables the installation and execution of third-party apps, enhancing the device's functionality.

User Interface and Interaction

Humane AI PIN's user interface is developed around the ideals of simplicity and intuitiveness. The lack of a traditional screen needs a new approach to information presentation and user interaction.

The interface relies mostly on voice commands and gestures to explore menus, access information, and control various functionalities. The device's inbuilt AI constantly analyzes the user's speech and actions, offering contextual responses and anticipating requirements.

Key features of the user interface include:

• **Natural Language Processing:** Enables direct and intuitive contact with the AI assistant via natural language commands and questions.

• **Contextual Awareness:** The AI modifies its responses and recommendations based on the user's current condition, location, and past interactions.

• **Multimodal Input:** Supports a combination of voice commands, gestures, and haptic feedback for a natural and intuitive user experience.

• **Customizable Settings:** Users can tailor the interface by modifying voice response settings, notification choices, and gesture controls.

Voice Assistant Integration

Humane AI PIN contains a sophisticated voice assistant that serves as the major focus for user engagement. This assistant leverages advanced speech recognition and natural language processing skills to interpret user requests and offer accurate responses.

Key functionalities of the voice assistant include:

• **Voice Recognition and Synthesis:** Recognizes user's voice instructions and provides natural-sounding responses.

• **Task Management:** Allows users to schedule reminders, set alarms, and manage calendars with voice commands.

• **Information Access:** Provides real-time access to weather updates, news headlines, and other important information.

• **Application Control:** Enables users to launch and control programs with voice commands.

• **Personalized Recommendations:** offers actions and information based on user interests and habits.

App Ecosystem and Compatibility

Humane AI PIN offers an open-platform design that allows for the development and installation of third-party applications. This enables users to personalize their experience and access a wide range of capabilities beyond the essential functionality supplied by the device.

The app ecosystem is carefully selected to ensure compatibility and high-quality user experiences. Developers can leverage a dedicated SDK to create applications specifically designed for the device's unique features and operating system.

Software Updates and Security

Humane AI PIN undergoes regular software updates that provide new features, improve performance, and resolve any security concerns. These updates are provided wirelessly and can be installed automatically or manually by the user.

The gadget prioritizes user data security and implements comprehensive security features, including data encryption, secure connection protocols, and frequent security audits. Users have full control over their data and can modify privacy settings to suit their experience.

Chapter 6: Communication and Productivity Features

Humane AI PIN helps individuals to communicate successfully and manage their daily duties easily. This chapter digs into the device's communication and productivity functions, analyzing how it supports effective communication, streamlines workflows, and boosts overall productivity.

Voice and Text Communication

Humane AI PIN's voice-first approach revolutionizes the way we communicate with our loved ones and colleagues. The device allows for:

• **Hands-free calling:** Initiate and receive calls with easy voice commands, removing the need to hold a smartphone.

• **Voice messaging:** Dictate and transmit text messages without typing, ensuring efficient and convenient communication.

• **Real-time voice translation:** Communicate successfully with folks speaking different languages with real-time voice translation.

• **Text-to-speech and speech-to-text:** Convert text communications to voice and vice versa, giving accessibility and convenience in diverse scenarios.

Call Management and Screening

Humane AI PIN delivers intelligent call management features that help users prioritize their interactions. These features include:

• **Caller ID with voice announcement:** Identify incoming callers without needing to look at a screen.

• **Call screening:** Filter calls based on established rules or contact information.

• **Call recording:** Record critical phone calls for future reference.

• **Call forwarding and voicemail:** Manage incoming calls and access voicemail messages conveniently.

Email and Calendar Management

Humane AI PIN interacts easily with common email and calendar programs. This allows users to:

• **Check and handle emails:** View, reply to, and delete emails hands-free using voice commands.

• **Create and manage calendar events**: Add, amend, and delete appointments and events with voice commands.

• **Receive calendar notifications:** Get reminders for upcoming events immediately on the smartphone.

• **Sync with various accounts:** Easily link the device with numerous email and calendar accounts.

Productivity Tools and Applications

Humane AI PIN is a collection of productivity solutions aimed at streamlining daily chores and boosting efficiency. These include:

• **Notes and reminders:** Dictate and organize notes, make to-do lists, and set reminders to stay on top of tasks.

• **Dictionary and language study:** Access a comprehensive dictionary for quick reference and employ language learning modules to improve language skills.

• **Unit conversion and computations:** Perform rapid calculations and unit conversions with voice commands.

• **Integration with third-party apps:** Connect with productivity apps such as Evernote, Todoist, and Trello for extra functionality.

Collaboration and Workflow Management

Humane AI PIN facilitates communication and enhances workflow management through features like:

• **Shared calendars and notes:** Collaborate with colleagues or team members on shared calendars and notes.

• **Task delegation and tracking:** Assign tasks to team members and monitor their progress.

• **Real-time document editing:** Edit and collaborate on documents in real-time with peers.

- **Meeting transcription and note-taking:** Record and transcribe meetings to capture key points and action items.

Chapter 7: Information and Knowledge Management

Humane AI PIN is not merely a communication and productivity tool; it also acts as a powerful platform for information and knowledge management. This chapter analyzes how the gadget supports users in obtaining, organizing, and utilizing information effectively, transforming the way they study, work, and make decisions.

Real-time Information Access and Updates

Humane AI PIN enables rapid access to a large array of real-time information, including:

• **News headlines and breaking news updates:** Stay informed about current events and breaking news through audio updates and projected summaries.

• **Weather predictions and real-time weather updates:** Plan your day and remain updated about weather conditions through personalized voice forecasts and predicted weather maps.

• **Traffic updates and navigation assistance:** Get real-time traffic updates and turn-by-turn navigation directions straight on the device.

• **Financial updates and market analysis:** Access real-time stock quotations, market news, and personalized financial insights.

Personal Knowledge Organization

Humane AI PIN helps people to tailor their information experience and organize knowledge effectively with features such as:

• **Customizable information feeds:** Create personal information feeds by selecting preferred news sources, subjects, and interests.

• **Note-taking and voice recording:** Capture essential points from information sources and meetings with voice recording and transcription capabilities.

• **Personalized search and filtering:** Search for specific information or filter information based on your preferences and context.

• **Contextual knowledge aggregation:** The AI assistant gathers and provides relevant information depending on the user's current circumstances, location, and interests.

Contextual Awareness and Personalized Recommendations

Humane AI PIN goes beyond merely showing information; it recognizes the user's context and delivers personalized recommendations based on their needs and preferences. This includes:

• **Anticipatory information delivery:** The device anticipates the user's wants and proactively delivers relevant information before it is asked.

• **Contextual reminders:** Receive personalized reminders depending on location, time, or past interactions.

• **Suggested actions and next steps:** The AI assistant offers actions and next steps depending on the current context and information available.

• **Personalized learning and skill development:** The gadget provides learning materials and personalized training programs according to the user's interests and goals.

Search and Retrieval Capabilities

Humane AI PIN's extensive search and retrieval features help users find the information they need quickly and efficiently. This includes:

• **Natural language search:** Search for information using natural language queries, reducing the need for sophisticated keywords.

• **Contextual search:** The AI assistant recognizes the context of the search query and gives relevant results based on user history and preferences.

• **Multimodal search:** Combine voice commands, gestures, and text to refine searches and filter down results.

• **Integrated search across several platforms:** Search for information across different services and applications connected to the device.

Chapter 8: Privacy and Security Considerations

As with any technology that collects and maintains personal data, privacy, and security are essential issues for users of Humane AI PIN. This chapter goes into these key features, analyzing how the gadget resolves privacy concerns and preserves user data from illegal access and exploitation.

Data Privacy Protection and User Control

Humane AI PIN promotes user data privacy and empowers people to govern their information through numerous features:

• **Transparent data collection and usage practices:** The device explicitly notifies users about the data it gathers, how it is used, and with whom it is shared.

• **Granular privacy settings:** Users can choose the sorts of data collected and manage how their information is used for personalization and advertising.

• **Limited data storage:** The gadget keeps limited personal data on-device, decreasing the possible impact of security breaches.

• **Offline functionality:** Many features work offline, protecting privacy even when not connected to a network.

• **Data deletion and opt-out options:** Users can request deletion of their data and opt out of data sharing at any time.

Secure Communication Protocols and Encryption

Humane AI PIN implements robust security methods to protect user data during communication:

• **End-to-end encryption:** All data transported between the device and the cloud is encrypted, ensuring secrecy and protecting against eavesdropping.

• **Secure communication methods:** The device leverages secure communication protocols such as HTTPS and TLS to ensure data integrity and prevent unauthorized access.

• **Regular security audits:** The device and platform undergo regular security assessments to discover and address problems swiftly.

Transparent Data Handling Practices

Humane AI PIN aspires for transparency in its data processing practices:

• **Clear privacy policy:** A clear and simple privacy policy defines the device's data collecting, storage, and usage regulations.

• **Regular communication about data practices:** Users are regularly informed about changes to data handling practices through updates and notifications.

• **Access to user data:** Users have the right to access their data stored on the device and cloud platforms.

Responsible AI Ethics and Guidelines

Humane AI PIN conforms to ethical criteria and concepts for responsible research and use of AI:

• **Fairness and non-discrimination:** The gadget is meant to operate fairly and non-discriminatory towards all users.

• **Transparency and explainability:** The AI algorithms are designed to be transparent and explainable, allowing people to understand how decisions are made.

• **Accountability and user control:** Users have control over how their data is used by the AI algorithms and may hold them accountable for their outputs.

• **Human monitoring and review:** Human experts oversee the development and deployment of the AI algorithms, guaranteeing responsible use and limiting possible hazards.

Chapter 9: Future of Humane AI PIN and AI Wearables

Humane AI PIN is a pioneering invention in the world of wearable technology, delivering a glimpse into the future of human-computer interaction and AI integration in our daily lives. This chapter digs into the intriguing potential of this technology, exploring the projected improvements in AI wearables and their impact on society.

Potential Advancements in AI Wearable Technology

The future of AI wearables has great promise for further advances, including:

• **Enhanced Processing Power and AI Capabilities:** More powerful processors and advanced AI algorithms will enable more sophisticated features, like real-time language translation, personalized health and fitness coaching, and immersive augmented reality experiences.

• **Enhanced battery Life and Energy Efficiency:** Technological developments will lead to enhanced battery life, addressing a major problem for wearable devices and permitting uninterrupted use throughout the day.

• **Seamless Integration with the Internet of Things (IoT):** AI wearables will effortlessly integrate with other smart devices within the IoT ecosystem, enabling tailored automation of homes, workplaces, and other surroundings.

• **Advanced Biometric Sensors and Health Monitoring:** More sophisticated biosensors will measure a larger range of health and wellness data, delivering individualized insights and preventive health suggestions.

• **Fashionable and customizable Design:** AI wearables will expand beyond their practical functions, becoming more beautiful and customizable to adapt to individual preferences and aesthetics.

Impact of AI Wearables on Society and Daily Life

These breakthroughs in AI wearables will have a major impact on society and daily life, including:

• **Enhanced Productivity and Efficiency:** AI wearables will streamline daily tasks, boost productivity, and deliver real-time information and help, empowering individuals to achieve their goals more successfully.

• **Individualized healthcare and wellness management:** AI wearables will enable continuous health monitoring, individualized interventions, and proactive health management, leading to better well-being and decreased healthcare expenditures.

• **Accessibility and inclusion for individuals with disabilities:** AI wearables will offer assistive technology and individualized support, boosting accessibility and inclusivity for those with impairments.

• **Enhanced learning and skill development:** AI wearables will customize the learning experience, offering real-time feedback and adaptive learning aids to maximize skill acquisition and information retention.

• **New types of social engagement and entertainment:** AI wearables will support new forms of social connection, immersive entertainment experiences, and enhanced cooperation in both virtual and physical locations.

Ethical Considerations and Responsible Development

As AI wearables become increasingly integrated into our lives, ethical considerations and responsible development procedures become crucial. These include:

• Balancing user privacy and data security with the potential benefits of AI technologies.

• Ensuring algorithmic fairness and non-discrimination, minimizing bias, and encouraging inclusivity.

• Addressing the psychological consequences and addiction concerns linked with constant connectivity and AI-driven interactions.

• Promoting openness and user control over data collection, usage, and decision-making processes.

• Developing ethical principles and regulations for responsible AI development and deployment.

Humane AI PIN's Role in Shaping the Future of Wearables

Humane AI PIN has established itself as a pioneer in the field of AI wearables, creating a new standard for user-centric design, privacy-conscious development, and unique functionalities. As the technology continues to evolve, the Humane AI PIN is poised to play a crucial role in determining the future of wearables, ensuring that they are produced and deployed ethically, responsibly, and for the benefit of humanity.

The future of AI wearables is loaded with potential. By harnessing the power of AI and addressing ethical considerations appropriately, these technologies have the potential to alter the way we live, work, learn, and interact with the world around us. Humane AI PIN acts as a beacon for this future, paving the way for a new era of human-centered technology that empowers individuals and increases our collective well-being. As we embrace the possibilities of AI wearables, it is vital to prioritize ethical development, responsible use, and human-centric design principles to guarantee that this technology serves as a force for good, encouraging progress and prosperity for all.

Conclusion

This book has taken you on a tour around the world of Humane AI PIN, covering its novel features, functionality, and potential impact on our lives. We have seen how this gadget overcomes the constraints of standard wearables, giving a unique blend of communication, productivity, information access, augmented reality, and wellness management functions.

As we near the conclusion of our exploration, it is crucial to think about the profound ramifications of the Humane AI PIN and similar technologies. This book has not only offered an overview of features; it has uncovered a new era of human potential, where technology serves as a tool for empowerment, advancement, and connection.

Key Takeaways:

• Humane AI PIN symbolizes a paradigm leap in human-computer interaction. By promoting natural language interfaces and voice commands, it offers a more intuitive and user-friendly experience, decreasing reliance on screens and cultivating a more thoughtful approach to technology.

• This ingenious device helps us to achieve more with less effort. Its productivity features ease daily chores, while access to real-time information and personalized recommendations enhance decision-making and problem-solving.

• Humane AI PIN alters the way we access and interact with information. Its powerful search skills and contextual awareness enable us to discover the information we need quickly and efficiently, while augmented reality overlays offer immersive and interactive experiences.

• This technology holds enormous potential for increasing our well-being and health. By recording workout data, monitoring sleep habits, and delivering individualized health suggestions, Humane AI PIN empowers us to take charge of our health and well-being.

• Beyond individual benefits, Humane AI PIN provides chances for cooperation, learning, and connection. Its communication and sharing features promote seamless contact with others, while its individualized learning tools and AR elements encourage cooperation and exploration.

Looking Forward:

The journey with Humane AI PIN has only just begun. As this technology grows and integrates more effortlessly into our lives, we should expect to witness even more dramatic developments and revolutions. These include:

• Enhanced AI capabilities: More powerful AI algorithms will enable deeper personalization, context-aware decision-making, and increasingly sophisticated augmented reality experiences.

• Seamless connection with the Internet of Things: Humane AI PIN will become a key point for managing smart homes, workplaces, and other connected areas, boosting automation and ease.

• Tailored healthcare and preventative medicine: Advanced medical sensors and AI-powered diagnostics will enable continuous health monitoring, tailored risk assessments, and early detection of health concerns.

• New kinds of human-computer interaction: We may anticipate seeing more natural and intuitive methods to connect with technology, including brain-computer interfaces and haptic feedback for a more immersive and sensory experience.

• Focus on ethical development and responsible usage: As AI technology grows increasingly powerful, guaranteeing its responsible development and use will be important to addressing potential concerns and promoting a positive future for humanity.

Humane AI PIN provides a great instrument for unlocking our full potential as individuals and as a collective. By embracing this technology and its promise, we may usher in a new era of human-centered innovation, where technology empowers us to do more, live healthier, and connect with the world in meaningful ways. As we move forward, let us remember that technology is not a replacement for human connection and interaction; rather, it is a tool that can be utilized to enhance our lives, augment our experiences, and link us with the people and things that matter most.

www.ingramcontent.com/pod-product-compliance
Lightning Source LLC
Chambersburg PA
CBHW071305050326
40690CB00011B/2538

* 9 7 9 8 8 7 1 1 2 0 9 8 9 *